INCANDESCENT VISIONS
BY LEE HUDSPETH

Copyrighted Material

INCANDESCENT VISIONS

Copyright © 2019 by Lee Hudspeth. All Rights Reserved.

Cover art by Preston M. Smith, *Elements and Dreamscapes*, pmsartwork.com. Copyright © 2019 by Preston M. Smith.

No part of this publication may be reproduced, stored in a retrieval system or transmitted, in any form or by any means—electronic, mechanical, photocopying, recording or otherwise—without prior written permission from the publisher, except for the inclusion of brief quotations in a review.

For information about this title or to order other books and/or electronic media, contact the publisher:

Lee Hudspeth

409 N. Pacific Coast Highway
Suite 145
Redondo Beach, CA 90277

leehudspeth.com

info@leehudspeth.com

HARDCOVER: 978-1-7334364-0-3
SOFTCOVER: 978-1-7334364-1-0
eBOOK: 978-1-7334364-2-7

Cover and interior design by 1106 Design

Printed in the United States of America

DEDICATION

For Liz, Aaron and Tate

CONTENTS

Preface 6

Acknowledgements 7

Chapter 1: Dear Reader, Hello 9

Chapter 2: Reflections 15

Chapter 3: It's Getting Dark in Here 25

Chapter 4: Motion. 33

Chapter 5: A Celebration of All Things 39

Afterword: Author's Comments 56

PREFACE

I am curious about creativity. One of the main themes in this collection of poems is my exploration of the nature of creativity. Where does it originate? Does it change over the course of our lives, or do we change while our creative energy remains present but fluctuating between obscured, enhanced or somewhere between?

In these poems I also explore nostalgia; how our experiences shape us; our place in the world and the choice we have at any given moment to change ourselves. I'm intrigued by our ability to observe ourselves, to think about thinking (metacognition), and to change our habits, even our underlying way of viewing the world. I believe that the capacity to change oneself is suppressed by our culture, or maybe it's just too much work, I don't know for sure. But I'm convinced it can be done. First, observe and take responsibility for our personal history and experiences. Second, notice the patterns in that history. Third, choose one's path forward, and work to encourage the good and minimize the undesirable habits and views.

The title of this book and one poem within it — "Where Before There Were Incandescent Visions" — share the phrase "incandescent visions." When I first came up with that poem's title, it represented a theme of passionate (incandescent) curiosity and the yearning to express oneself, and so the nucleus of that poem's title also belongs in the book's title. As other poems joined the book, more themes emerged: storytelling, travel, perspective, inspiration, nature, memorials, the challenges of dark times, the arc of our lives, self-improvement, celebration, love, among others... I hope you find inspiration here.

ACKNOWLEDGEMENTS

As I sat down to write this section, I was tempted to roll the master tape all the way back. Did it start with a toddler-sized portable turntable and a collection of 45 rpm records? Books being read to me by my parents? Church choir and youth band; Neil Young and a plethora of musicians who inspired me in high school; a mystical yet very real farm in Maine; the 1970s in their entirety; friends made near to home and in faraway places... I think I see a thread. I appreciate all the people I've met along the way who encouraged my curiosity and creativity. The feeling is mutual.

Many thanks to everybody who helped.

Eloise and George Hudspeth, my mom and dad, for countless acts of generosity, kindness and support.

Aaron Harsch-Hudspeth for editing this book and excellent advice throughout.

Alex Lockwood, who recorded, mixed and mastered the audio book (Studio 637, Hermosa Beach, California). Thanks to Alex, Claire Davenport and Kevin Yamada for audio production suggestions, encouragement and support.

Preston M. Smith, for his imaginative, vibrant and inspiring paintings.

Beta readers Jeff Baker, Jim Cowherd, Mary Cowherd, Stephanie Cowherd, Claire Davenport, Liz Harsch, Aaron Harsch-Hudspeth, Tate Harsch-Hudspeth, Jeff Hromadka, Alex Lockwood, Miles Pritzkat, Audrey Wertz and Kevin Yamada.

Angelo Finaldi and Danielle Charland, who embraced the corner table and then our hearts. You cheered me on from the beginning.

Dr. Scott C. Fraser, for everything.

CHAPTER 1: DEAR READER, HELLO

CHAPTER 1 PROLOGUE

This chapter is a first encounter between us. An introduction. I want to begin with poetry that I was inspired to write while traveling. I find that when I'm far from the comforts of home, I gain a new and fresh perspective about what is important to me.

The Point of Four Winds
Wanderlust
Exquisite Ercolano
Farewell Italy

THE POINT OF FOUR WINDS

One is Day, to remember
Two is Night, to caress
Three is Rain, to bless
Four is Cosmology, to engender

Bringing me tolerance
The four winds encourage clarity
Resist the hubris of me
Upend my elitist poverty
Reject the paralysis of incuriosity

Missing the point altogether
With my own tempest
I am guilty
So I work to be kinder
The six breaths and all the rest
Let it go, fratello[1]

---

1   Italian for "brother"

WANDERLUST

Cast askew, bare before me, hovering
A collection of cosmic tricks like these
Rocks, sky, clouds and trees
Is what I really see, real?

Others before me have asked,
"How does it feel?"
Silly cliché, oh sleight of hand
Waved up by a stardust factory in a singular plan

Maps at a scale beyond my grasp
But who else will map these ethereal strings
Of time and space and wandering souls
Tiny yet so, so grand
Is it cliché or sleight of hand?

Trails that lure me from peak to beach
Scaled down to be within our reach
My footsteps echo on these paths
My eyes see rocks, sky, clouds and trees
My eyes see

EXQUISITE ERCOLANO

Our roots are entwined with so many languages
I'm rooted to one, but I hear the many
As things progress, I climb to the canopy
These languages, they drift up and sing sweetly to me
They smell of the sea and magic, tinged with potentiality
Grains of dust from the earth's layered intricacies, circulate history
And, it's okay

Swaying, the wind ushers memories to me like precious gifts
I open the package and peer inside
A smooth emerald pebble, a blue feather,
    an archipelago of musical notes
"Ah ha," I say aloud, "that's the way"
So simple, eh?
I'm greeting a nice surprise
Grand, formed, transparent
The horizon, an interior view, humility, a laughter that awakes...
Intrigued, I inhale

FAREWELL ITALY

Looking down, I weep
The last train out of the stazione
Your bountiful hospitality
History ancient, splendid, brutal, sublime
Green landscape surrounding the revered ruins of time and sacrifice

CHAPTER 2: REFLECTIONS

CHAPTER 2 PROLOGUE

This chapter touches on themes such as the arc of our lives (the transitions from childhood to adolescence to adulthood), inspiration, perspective, nature and the yearning for self-improvement. Two of this chapter's poems are memorials, reflecting on the death of my mother and a friend.

For Eric, Thank You
Inspire Me Again
Framework
Crescent Moon
Cornerstones
Mom

FOR ERIC, THANK YOU

Yet another direction, now
A small hill under a clear blue sky
A boisterous, verdant valley
Country gravel lane with tree branches intertwined overhead
A patina of sea salt glistening on jumbled rocks,
    momentarily free of the tide
Years ago, Eric, before I met you, a shimmering furnace-hot wind
    enveloped me in Scottsdale, Arizona
That wind locked me into place
It embedded itself into my DNA
I welcomed it in, as you welcomed me
That wind liberated me
It carries me forward to this day, and
It remains as a bridge to something ineffable
Emerging landscapes, from the distant horizon
    into the palm of my hand
Leading anywhere and everywhere
Then back and around again
I want to be on that barely perceptible, delicate, secret path
I... *must*... be on it
So that I can step off and back on again
So that I can absolutely connect
Is it enough to be still?
Enough to be in motion?
Yes
To resonate

—*in memory of Eric Bolt*

INSPIRE ME AGAIN

A hundred different ways this could go
It's a simple story to be cherished
From a handful of words on a folded piece of paper
That a friend shyly gave me years ago

We were young and inspired then
The way high school kids can be
Nothing wrong with that, Lord no
"Times gone by" is a fine place to go

It took courage for my friend
Sitting alone with paper and pen
To compose her innermost thoughts
She handed them to me then
The years rolled by, now I'm inspired again

Hidden away in a quiet dusty drawer
Kindly kept safe by my father
For those many years
He always valued remembrances
Here, a handful of words on a folded piece of paper

FRAMEWORK

A framework opens up
Four corners, a stretched white canvas, a tiny red dot
The white dunes ripple away
Radiating like the heat of time

You ask me, "Why?"
I tell you, "It's the dot."
You shout back, "No it's not!"
Whatever I come up with
Whatever I say
Boxes me in
I don't feel it yet, anyway

I hold the framework in my hands
The framework embraces me in return
It is a portal to other lands
People, dreams and possibilities
The neat trick is out beyond the edges
The realm of Peter Pan
"Second star to the right and straight on till morning"
No hesitation now, I know where I'm going

You've been in my head all this time
I only needed a nudge to find my line
On the face of the wave that only I can see
Where and how I carve the line is entirely up to me

CRESCENT MOON

Floating effortlessly in the early night sky
Framed by an occasional cloud
She captured our ancestors' imagination
Only two hundred thousand years have gone by

Tonight a crescent moon is rising
With no regard for human trivialities
She's not impressed by our 24-7 data streaming
By our relentless "who what when where whys"

The TV over the bar does not hang like that
Instead
It's a shameless firehose of blaring, glaring fake news sharing
Politics and posturing
Seductive social media feeding frenzy

Tonight's crescent moon shines with inspiration
Antidote to trickster corporations
That compel us to be vain heroes
Every minute, hour, day
To scratch an itch that never goes away
The crescent moon patiently has her say

CORNERSTONES

Brick by brick
It might be just another trick
Lest we forget
Dare we remember
The stones take us back
We meander and careen from one to the other
Sometimes faithfully
More often mistakenly
Can we afford to be cornered so cleverly?
Victims of our own structure
Digging through the ruins, we fluctuate
Searching for the cornerstones
Upending the sins
I was bullied
You were lied to
She was diminished
He was homogenized
We were all told to BE QUIET
Those are the rotten corners
Leave them to their decline
Grain by grain
Replace the pain
Tie in to the emergent picture
The latticework of new and vibrant anchors

MOM

A leaf is poised, unaware
Against the backdrop of the twilight sky
A complicated, busy street
       town
              continent
                      earth
Surrounds and suspends the tree that hosts the leaf

Isn't that the way it is?
That is precisely the way it is with so many things human
Immeasurably large and dynamic
Sometimes it's easier to step back and be right here
On the sidewalk
Looking up at the leaf and the indigo umbrella sky
As the early-evening stars hover, peeking through the haze
Coming into focus

The way our lives have come into focus
From the moment of our birth until now
Loping along at the pace of a child growing up
Under the watchful, loving eye of a mother

I encourage you to remember
Back to the magical time of being poised yourself
Against the backdrop of your mother's umbrella sky
On the verge of your next step, word, smile, question
Recall the exquisite simplicity of her encouragement and love

The power of those early gestures
Gifts from mother to son and daughter
Gestures that radiate undiminished through our lives

Today we lope along at a different pace
Adulthood, middle age, your moniker of choice
Perhaps your mother is now a memory
So, look back and around
Take strength from immersing yourself in those experiences
Propagate them along your own life's arc
The ripples are there
All we have to do is look
Right, Mom?
We honor them

—In memory of Eloise Hughes Hudspeth

CHAPTER 3: IT'S GETTING DARK IN HERE

CHAPTER 3 PROLOGUE

Darkness. Despair. Self-doubt. Fear. Trouble. We've all had these feelings, to one degree or another. In this chapter I reflect on dark times that I've experienced personally.

The poem "I Don't Want To" warrants a special mention. I initially considered it to be too negative and too raw to publish. I felt that it was overly strident, militant and critical; as though I was saying, "Hey, I'm not a jerk but everyone else is." My son Aaron felt strongly that I should publish it. He said it's a good thing to be outraged at the appropriate time and that readers will relate to my frustration with authoritarian people and institutions. Alex Lockwood, the audio engineer on this book, winked and reminded me several times, "Lee, the fact that you *don't want to* publish a poem entitled "I Don't Want To," of course you *have to* publish it." There you go. The lesson is: Listen to yourself and listen to your advisors.

Bloated Rodeo
I Don't Want To
4:00 am
Broken
Where Before There Were Incandescent Visions
Stronger

BLOATED RODEO

I hear the siren song
Calling me to the bloated rodeo
It's a bar fight don't you know
Starring my precious little frontal lobe and super-ego

Rooting around
Where I know I shouldn't go down
What is this, under the mattress
Some new kind of kiss
Keep it simple stupid
Oh it's much too late for that

Looking sideways, down, all around
To catch a glimpse of who's in town
Petty, pretty, oh man, it makes me giddy
Better sink my teeth into another martini

Where have I been revered lately?
I desperately want to hear what you have to say
Did anyone take my picture?
When does the next bloated rodeo play?

I DON'T WANT TO

That is your way
Not my way
Rocking the boat, jerking everyone's chain
Do you even understand that your pleasure is our pain?

Too loud, too soft, no in-between
No compromise, no daylight
Not even a point of view
When the sky falls through
Who will be left for you to beat down?
I will be long gone
Although drenched in your squalid tirade
I'll be leading the rebels on an upside parade

Why don't you try some self-appraisal
Can you do that?
I doubt you can settle
For the truth underneath your woeful hat

Changing lanes to beat a time
Go ahead and try it if it eases your mind
I'll be under the surface hosting my own sublime
Watch me saunter right on through to the promised land
I'm hanging back at the end of the line
Where thoughts are my own and they drift in kind
So blissfully slow, there is Anywhere and Everywhere to go

4:00 AM

When I clear my mind
The outcome is not what I expected
Shards careening, deflected
Where are the demons of my demise?
Where are the angels of my ascension?
I'll tell you where!

It's 4:00 a.m. on the outside
Angels and demons lounge under the cafeteria's harsh lights
Maybe they'll have a food fight
While I watch, disembodied and paralyzed, from the inside

Is it the wiring?
If they're supposed to be pawns in the chess game of my life
The one where I am King, at least for a day
Then something has gone badly astray

BROKEN

Externalities: confirmed
Boundary conditions: conceptualized
Projections: anticipated
Smooth reflective surface: unbroken
Dendrites: collect and convey
Algorithms: recursive and questioning
Outcome: engage and expand

Wait

Risk assessment, jittery, prevails unchecked
Bell curve,
    standard deviations,
        functions branch to miscalculation
Re-examine
Normal is, normal is not
A halting precipitates
Immobility

Broken

Step

One

Learn

Stillness emerges as a way to enfold, all things
Fractures, crevasses, burden the whole
Undeterred regardless
Brokenness confounds the observer, and transforms elegantly

WHERE BEFORE THERE WERE INCANDESCENT VISIONS

A roiling center
A profusion of energy
Emits lines, waves and shapes that become dreams
Unstoppable
Embedded in a human frame

Rituals impose and scaffold a shroud around
That surely extinguishes the light and heat and yearnings
On
Then off
Just like that

Sol, the sun, our star, my soul
Ambushed and cloaked
By the insidious overlord whom we designed and promoted
    to the post
An unfolding social construct
Built upon conformity, suppression and doubt

The star within, now concealed by an ironclad shell
Opaque
Dark
Cold
Nothing escapes
Where before there were incandescent visions
For all to see

Tear it all down
Undo the damage done
Restart the core
Rekindle the light and heat
That is you

STRONGER

When what once was within reach, is no longer
They say, "What doesn't kill you makes you stronger"
Sometimes that just isn't true
If along the way you falter
And no one's there to offer you
Shelter and a glimmer of hope
When the sky rains down darker
It's hard to see much farther
Than the small circle of despair that surrounds you

You don't know it yet, motion is your salvation
Take one more step in any direction
Strength floods in long after it's over
The demons grind you down with your own thoughts
But they don't know shit about the future

In the moment, it's not about the moment
Ghostly priors, messy entanglements
Hanging like links of a heavy chain

Maybe it's best to not look back?
I'm not sure about that
I do know the attack came entirely from within
Keep my chin up and all that
Forward-thinking stuff
I'll use that as a lever for onward

I confess I still look over my shoulder
To see the smoldering glow of what went down
Eventually the curvature will win
I'll take one step at a time until then

CHAPTER 4: MOTION

CHAPTER 4 PROLOGUE

Where have you been? Where are you now? Where are you headed? Fair questions. I'm sure we have all asked ourselves, "How the hell did I get here, exactly?" In this chapter's poems I take a look at how we move around in the world (sometimes engaging and sometimes withdrawing); those fascinating pivot points in our lives where one thing or person or gesture sends us tumbling off in a different direction; landscapes of the places that shape us, even long after we leave them; and how we cope with the people we care about as they weave in and out of our lives.

Going Downtown
I Threw My Maps and Journals Away
Backward
Warehouse of Dreams

GOING DOWNTOWN

I won't go downtown
For another round
Just to be around the crowd
'Cause it is much too loud

Get to know me, man
I'm probably way too proud
And anyhow
I don't need to talk right now
No holding back, my main man Jack
Gonna show you glitterati, I'll be back

I THREW MY MAPS AND JOURNALS AWAY

Her long brown hair
Made the summertime flow
Her shining smile and the sparkle in her eyes
Told me everything I wanted to know

I threw my maps and journals away
Sadly, I couldn't find that place today
A half-remembered mantra
An un-answered question
Just a few words could've changed our direction

She lived in a house alongside a backcountry road
Broken asphalt, overgrowth, the smell of the nearby sea
I walked that road and those moody forest trails
Countless times, now a distant memory
She sure could have educated me

BACKWARD

Pumping gas in my car
I see a woman on a bicycle
On the sidewalk of a bustling city street
In front of the gas station

She pedals slowly backward and coasts to a stop
Then she pedals forward, and waits
She repeats herself, as if pacing
Like the sidewalk is her carpeted hallway for forgetting

In one hand, a cigarette
An iced tea in the other
All the while, pedaling backward
Trying to stay balanced, not so well
(I'm not always so well balanced either)

A large handbag hangs precariously over her shoulder
Socks, but no shoes
She is very sunburned
Where has she been today?
Where is she going?
Her movements seem counterproductive
Who am I to say?
How did these patterns develop?
Is today my lucky day?

I can't move, but she does
Eventually she pedals off into the distance
Swallowed up by the oblivious traffic
What is her life story?
Where are her shoes, goddamn it?

WAREHOUSE OF DREAMS

The grocery warehouse smells of sundries
Cardboard and tobacco
              Rising
       Rising
Rising
On pallets and shelves
Waiting for deliverance, just as we were

Idle chatter floats above the machinery's din
Elders pontificating
Youngsters skeptical, yawning behind hands
The cigarette-tax stamping machine cl-cl-clanks along,
    mindlessly devouring an endless supply of cartons
We were innocent, at the time

Streets aplenty, in this small rural town
Some are paved, some are dirt
Winding their way to unkempt graveyards
Right up to the very edge of unimaginable mortality
Colliding with a golden, carefree, insect-buzzing summer day

Abandoned homes collapsing
Down into the weeds and scrub
Anxious to win
No condominiums here

Small creeks full of fishing holes
Passageways to yesterday
Smells and old photographs beckon me back
Summer after ever-shortening summer

CHAPTER 5: A CELEBRATION OF ALL THINGS

CHAPTER 5 PROLOGUE

I organized this chapter into two parts. The first part is a series of haiku, with no titles. (In the list below, the first line of each haiku serves as its pseudo-title.) I wrote each of these haiku to honor a loved one, an arrival, a departure or a place I visited. The word "celebration" in the chapter title has a connotation of "elevation," meaning that I'm looking at experiences we celebrate because they elevate and inspire us. This chapter concludes with three longer poems (not haiku). One, about music. The next, about goodbyes and a reminder to treasure our time with loved ones. The last, a love poem for my wife Liz.

HAIKU
Water over rocks
Deep green and mossy
Sunlight filtered blue
A student here now
Latitudinal
Arriving supple
Water flows softly
Notes like pearls arise
Rock wall, climbing free
Potential distributed
Road propels them north
Magic stone offered

NOT HAIKU
Speak to My Guitar
Goodbyes
I Draw My Strength from You

Water over rocks
Our love flows like that river
Onward unending

Deep green and mossy
Big Sur welcomes us to her
Sunlight weaves through trees

Sunlight filtered blue
Possibilities abound
Embracing next path

A student here now
A bridge crosses the ocean
Words will be exchanged

Latitudinal
This is where she lives right now
A radiant smile

Arriving supple
All positive swirling now
Adventures accrue

Water flows softly
Smiles despite the season's snow
Her dog jumps for joy

Notes like pearls arise
Levitation is applied
Village reaches up

Rock wall, climbing free
Power, stretch, taut, smooth release
Strata shimmering

Potential distributed
Rhythm of the now
Firm ground accepts fledgling steps

Road propels them north
Light glints off the vehicle
Family engages

Magic stone offered
A subatomic trembling
Mysteries abound

SPEAK TO MY GUITAR

I will speak to my guitar
And set out to find a melody
I think it will let me

Huddling together, working it out
Note by note
Measure by measure

We are carving a sculpture
Ingrained within the geometry of the fretboard
That which falls away, reveals the essence
A deep undercurrent of joy evokes the harmonics

The story and the melody converge
Into a shimmering cascade
Listen to what emerges!
Listen

GOODBYES

Tears trickle down your face
Slowly at first, then gaining pace
If you're walking, you stop cold
If thinking, now you cannot
If driving, you pull over and sit quite still
Your son or daughter or mother or lover or... someone
Is leaving

Your temples get tight, it hurts
Lowering your head, you surrender
Your hands cover your eyes
You can't control it, arms and shoulders trembling
The roaring inside your head is deafening
You feel it in your bones
Sad, angry, afraid, alone

You sigh
You wait
You steady yourself
Then you reminisce about goodbyes
Smell your loved one's hair
Laugh freely with them
Look into their eyes
And wink, knowingly
Squeeze their shoulder just so, gently
Let all of that reflect your love for them
A beacon of remembering

I DRAW MY STRENGTH FROM YOU

My soul mate comes from a place of grace
An unconstrained time and space
An open door, the light shines through
I draw my strength from you

From the beginning, I was falling…
Falling…
Into a love with no width, no depth, no limits
Into a love with only you

A gentle hand, now and then
You encourage me exactly when
I lose my way and I can't push on
My vision wavers, my thoughts come undone
Encouragement applied
It means so much
With these few words I have tried to convey
The many things I've neglected to say

AFTERWORD: AUTHOR'S COMMENTS

I considered providing notes in this section about each poem. I also considered not including any notes. I compromised by including notes for two of the longer poems. This way, you have some insight into my thoughts and process, without there being too much "behind the scenes" material here. I then have the option of posting notes for the other poems on my website LeeHudspeth.com or in other venues, for those of you who are interested.

I wrote "Broken" after reading another author's comments about his own work. Patrick Rothfuss is the author of the Kingkiller Chronicle series of novels. The first book in the series is *The Name of the Wind* followed by *The Wise Man's Fear*. I read the first two books in the series, then I read his novella *The Slow Regard of Silent Things*. After that, I read his notes about that book's main character Auri.

Auri is mentally "broken." I infer she has extreme obsessive-compulsive disorder (OCD) and maybe anthropophobia, which is a fear of people and society, therefore she feels alone. But other people (all of us?) are also broken, each in some unique way.

Rothfuss suggests that she has a latent strength that far surpasses that of her mentally "normal" teachers and mentors. Her strength is her ability to be still and to not interfere with the world, but instead to glide within it in a non-intrusive way. She can see the true underlying nature of objects and people, as in, she can discover and speak their "true name" (in his novels, Rothfuss explores the magical power of true names).

The book alludes to those who knew Auri, presumably before she had a traumatic experience or mental breakdown, and describes them thinking of her dismissively. But I, like Rothfuss, believe she can live a meaningful, even special, life despite or because of her flaws (her "brokenness"). "Brokenness confounds the observer, and transforms elegantly" — people don't pay much attention to other people and therefore typically misjudge them.

This novella also makes me think about our private lives, and how we tend to view the lives of other people as inherently "better" (especially in contemporary narcissism-driven, personality-curated social media culture). When in fact the lives of others may be far worse than ours. I took the concept of Auri as someone who is so over-powered by her OCD that she can be thought of as robotic, and I tried to write in a programming-code-like, algorithmic style. I chose to right-justify the lines of this poem on the printed page, to further highlight the sense of being out of the ordinary and different.

On the day that I had the idea for "Framework," I was sitting in a large auditorium to celebrate my niece Taylee's high school graduation. I was distracted by the noisy and boisterous scene until one of the speakers caught my attention. She told a story about giving her students a test. She handed out a plain white piece of paper with one red dot on it. The teacher told her students to write a response to that. Every student wrote about the red dot. None of them wrote about the surrounding whiteness, the texture of the paper, the classroom around them, the world around the classroom, etc. The point of the test being to encourage the students to look at the piece of paper *and* the context around it, instead of habitually focusing on the obvious.

The poem starts with a sort of meditation on what I see in my mind's eye when I imagine the sheet of paper and its tiny red dot. Then an imagined dialogue with the teacher, as if the narrator (me) is a high school student who "failed" the test and is not sure they understand the exercise — "I don't feel it yet, anyway." Then the narrator switches to me in current time, riffing on the idea of edges and boundaries, which prompted thoughts of Peter Pan, Neverland and youthful optimism. The star is a thematic reference to my fascination with cosmology. Somehow (too jarring, perhaps?) I switch metaphors from Neverland to surfing and, finally, self-determination. The framework represents both a person and a perspective. Whatever surrounds the framework could be perceived reality, that person's place in the world, the universe at large... I end the poem with the phrase "Where and how I carve the line is entirely up to me," a hint that each person uniquely sees their own framework and what lies beyond it, and determines their own fate.

ABOUT THE AUTHOR

Lee Hudspeth is a poet, musician, recording artist and fellow human being. He is the co-author of ten non-fiction books in the field of Information Technology. He has written articles for professional journals like *PC Computing* and *Office Computing*, and is the author of over one hundred articles in the online magazine *The Naked PC*, where he was co-founder and co-publisher. This is his first book of poetry. He lives in Hermosa Beach, California, with his wife, two sons and their cat. Find out more about Lee, his books and music at LeeHudspeth.com.

I HOPE YOU ENJOYED THIS BOOK. WOULD YOU DO ME A FAVOR?

Like all authors, I rely on online reviews to encourage future sales. Your opinion is invaluable. Would you take a few moments now to share your assessment of my book on Amazon or any other book review website you prefer? Your opinion will help the book marketplace become more transparent and useful to all. Thank you very much!

www.ingramcontent.com/pod-product-compliance
Lightning Source LLC
Chambersburg PA
CBHW071222070526
44584CB00019B/3125